Practical Activities for Children with Dyscalculia

Parents' Edition

Practical Activities for Children with Dyscalculia: Parents' Edition

By
Tony Attwood C.Ed., B.A., M.Phil. (Lond)

T1687

British Library Cataloguing in Publication Data.
A catalogue record for this book is available
from the British Library.

ISBN 1 86083 785 9

Published by First & Best in Education Ltd, Earlstrees Court, Earlstrees Road, Corby, Northants NN17 4HH
www.firstandbest.co.uk

Contents   Page

Dyscalculia on the internet

Information on the work of the Dyscalculia Group at First & Best is published on

www.dyscalculia.org.uk

If you have any queries about our work please email enquiries@dyscalculia.org.uk
or phone 01536 399004

Introduction

Since 1994 a team of researchers at First and Best has worked on providing materials that will help children and adults who have difficulties with spelling and/or with maths.

This book is the latest in a series of publications that arise from this project. All of our work for people who find maths particularly difficult follows the same approach.

It is clear to us that most people who have difficulty with maths suffer from not having fully learned and understood some of the most basic of mathematical concepts. Thus they are continuously attempting to deal with more advanced mathematical issues (such as, for example, the division of fractions) without first having understood simpler issues (such as division).

Everything in maths builds on everything else. If you don't learn the basics, you can't learn the next step. So if your child does not understand the concept of higher and lower numbers, then he or she cannot learn how to add. If a child does not know how to add it is very difficult to understand how your child might then learn how to multiply.

It is also clear that the best way to teach children who have a problem with maths is through using a multi-sensory approach. This approach means that the children say, hear, write and handle numbers simultaneously.

If this seems a little odd to you, it may be easiest to think of it as the exact opposite of you telling your child how to add up or subtract. In our approach the child handles counters and so when dealing with the number five the child physically handles five counters (touch) says "five", writes down "5" and hears you say "five".

Thus the child learns to relate the number "5" to something very real – something that has a name, and which can be touched and said.

Of course it may be that your child is already perfectly familiar with numbers as such, but gets confused when multiplying numbers. This book teaches multiplying numbers in the same way – by using counters, saying the numbers, hearing the numbers and so on.

Thus our approach is a dual system of maths in which the children use coloured counters together with the normal method of writing and solving maths problems. Through much of our material children therefore work on both the multi-sensory approach and the conventional approach, seeing that both give the same answer.

However as the problems get more complex the multi-sensory approach becomes less usable, and the advantages of the conventional approach become clearer. However if a problem arises which the child feels is incomprehensible when handled conventionally, she or he can always go back and use the multi-sensory approach.

We also believe that maths should be taught in short blocks of time, with each session building on what has gone before. Ten minutes for each session seems an ideal time to us, but this can be adjusted.

The materials in this book are not age specific – anyone who has difficulty with the five areas of maths we cover (number, addition, subtraction, multiplication, division) will be able to use the exercises in this book.

Although the book is divided into "days" you do not have to stick exactly to this formula. If the child is getting bored, tired or rebellious, stop the work and come back to it another time. If the child knows how to solve a problem very easily, move forward quickly to the next section.

Finding out where the problem is

The teachers at your child's school will be able to tell you if your child is slipping behind in maths, and if your child has a specific problem with certain types of maths. If you know that the problem is with division, and you are fairly sure that your child has no problem with subtraction, you can move straight on to that part of the book. If however you begin to feel that there are problems with addition, subtraction or multiplication, you will need to go back and try some exercises earlier in the book.

So if the teachers in your child's school state that she or he ought (at this stage in his/her schooling) to be able to multiply any two numbers under 20 together, then a logical place to start is at the opening of the multiplication section of this book. If however your child has problems following the multi-sensory approach, you might go back and look at the addition section of the book. If there is still a problem, then you should go back to the very start of this volume and consider whether the child does have a firm grasp of the concept of number.

On the other hand if the child gets four out of five answers right, it is normally perfectly safe to progress. But with anything less than this it is worth going back, or creating extra examples yourself, in order to ensure that all the learning is secure before you progress. If the child hits a mental block and can't get the answer at all, then never be afraid to try something simpler. Taking the idea of multiplying two numbers under 20, if this is causing a problem return to multiplying two numbers under 11. If there is still a problem you can go to the start of the multiplication section of this book. As before, if the child still has problems you might find it worth going back to the start of the book, but be ready to move forward at speed where it is clear that your child is fully conversant with the work.

Working day by day

It is important that you really do try and do some of this maths every day with your child. Of course there are always times when it is not so easy to do the maths – a night where the child goes swimming after school, has some other sporting activity, or is late back because of a visit to a relative, can put pressure on time. But do remember we are only looking for ten minutes work a day. It is a very short amount of time – especially when compared with the amount of time many children spend watching television each day.

You should aim to work with the child in a room where there are no distractions – such as a television, or the sound of the television. You should also try to avoid any situation in which your child is tempted to rush through the work – for example with a target of completing four questions by 7pm so that your child can then watch a programme on television. The aim should be ten minutes of meaningful concentrated work where the child is motivated to try his or her best for those ten minutes.

If the child is struggling it is important that you comment positively on the child's efforts and attempts to get things right. Do remember that it is quite likely that your child's problems with maths are due to the way your child's brain works – it is nothing to do with your child being lazy or stupid. The more you praise and reward your child the more he or she is going to work at maths. The more you criticise the child, the less likely the child will be able to do the maths.

You should also never tell the child that he or she is "no good at maths" – you must always be positive. If your child says, "I'll never get this right", you need to encourage the child, pointing out that many children have used this approach and learned how to do maths. Remind your child of how far she or he has already progressed and point out that further progress is not just possible, it is inevitable. You might also be tempted to admit that you had maths problems at school – but beware of this statement in case the child accepts it as an excuse. What we want the child to understand is that not being able to do basic maths does cause problems in later life, and a little work now will make life much easier in the future.

Look for uncertainties

Children who have dyscalculic problems don't get better by having answers told to them and being shown explanations. They must do the work themselves – they must take the problems and solve them. Because this is how we work throughout this book you can readily observe any uncertainties your child has. And once you have found them you can resolve the issue by going through the relevant section of this book in full.

Uncertainty is one of the learning tools of this book. Uncertainty means that a problem area is being located – and only through this can progress be made. Uncertainty is the start of progress, not a sign of past failure.

Make the learning fun

It is important that the ten minutes a day activity should not become something that the child hates. You should aim to be as upbeat and pleasant throughout the activities as possible. You should also participate as much as possible – you should certainly not set the child a problem and then leave the child while you do something else. This really does have to be ten minutes a day that you share with your child.

Rewards

It is a central part of the philosophy of this approach that your child is rewarded for participating every step of the way.

The rewards used are entirely a matter for you and might include:

- Playing a game
- Watching a TV programme
- Going to a particular event
- Having a friend round
- Having an extra story at bedtime
- Going to bed later
- Having a chocolate bar
- Going to a theme park.

This is not to suggest that your child should not have any fun without it being a reward – the reward should be an extra, in addition to normal every day life, in return for something concrete being done.

Some people suggest that rewards are like bribery, and that they are therefore wrong for children. Our view is different. We firmly believe that our lives are made up of things we will do for nothing – and things that we do for reward (in the adult world this often means money). Quite where the dividing line is between bribery and reward is difficult to say – if my employer says that he will pay me an extra £1000 this year if I will take on extra responsibility, is that a reward for my work or a way of bribing me to do another job?

The fact is that children exposed to reward systems often seem to learn more, and cope better with life in general, than children who have no reward system. They certainly seem to learn more and cope better than children who are exposed to a punishment based system.

We are very keen to hear your comments in relation to our approach to dyscalculia. You can reach us directly via email at mailto:enquiries@dyscalculia.org.uk. We welcome all comments about this book, and about dyscalculia in general, and we will make every effort to answer any questions you have about individual cases of dyscalculia, or about the topic in general.

Tony Attwood
Dyscalculia Team
September 2003

Section 1: Numbers, higher, lower

For some children the very concept of number is alien. This can be a big problem for adults, because for most of us it can seem so simple that it is inconceivable that a child doesn't know that 100 is greater than 99, or that 6 is greater than 3 - but if that is the case, then that is where work has to start.

In this first part of the book we are not looking at adding up or taking away, but at the meaning of the numbers themselves. What we need to do is to show the child that the symbol "6" represents six counters, six buttons, six people, and that "6" has a very real meaning that is different from "5" and indeed from all other numbers.

For the purposes of this book we are going to use counters to represent numbers as follows:

- Red = 1
- Blue = 10
- Green = 100
- Yellow = 1000

It is also helpful to have access to a range of blank cards (3" by 2" is a good size). As the work progresses children can use these either to help them build up the basic concept of number, or as memory aids to the representation of numbers mathematically. Thus it can be very useful for children who have difficulty with the whole concept of number to take blank cards and to draw on one side a set number of dots (for example six dots) and then on the other side write the number "6" and below that the word "six".

But please remember that you only need to work through this first section of the book if the child you are working with does not understand the basic concept of number. If the problem is with addition, subtraction, multiplication or division, rather than the basic concept of number itself, move on to the appropriate chapter.

Working through this chapter is not a pre-requisite for working with the rest of the book.

Finally, a reminder. We have divided up the activities below into days. However if there is too much work, or not enough for a child on one day, there is no need to adhere exactly to the day-by-day structure. If the child sails through one day's work there is nothing to stop you making a start on the next day's topic.

Part A: The meaning of numbers

Day 1.

1. You will need to obtain a large number of counters, of the type that you might have for playing Ludo or tiddlywinks. You will also need to have a pen or pencil and some paper for the child to use. Ideally obtain 20 red counters, 20 blue, 20 green and 20 yellow. These are the colours referred to in this book – however if you have other colours this will not be a problem.

2. Place two red counters down on the table and ask the child how many there are. The child must say the number, and write "2" on the paper as he/she says the answer. If there is real uncertainty with this, the child should also draw two counters and colour them in red, again saying two.

3. Continue this with other numbers up to 9, and going down to 0. The child must be able to recognise that "nothing" is a concept represented in maths by "0". Always use the same word for "0" – if the child says "zero" stay with "zero" from that point on.

Day 2.

1. Repeat the activities from yesterday with the numbers 7 and 8.

2. If the child cannot complete this task without error, go back to yesterday's work and continue with that until the child is secure in the concept of numbers.

3. If the child can undertake activity 1 above correctly, set out two groups of counters – one of 6 and one of 3. Ask the child to count each group and write down the number as before while she or he says the numbers.

4. Ask the child, which group has the most counters? If the child cannot do this, then you should ask the child to count the six out by physically moving them one at a time and counting up to six. Then do the same with the three. If the child still cannot see which is the largest, ask the child to count to six again moving the counters, and then point out that to get to the number six you actually went past the number 3.

5. If there is a still a problem with 6 and 3, go back to smaller numbers and try the work with 2 and 4.

6. As an additional aid to the child, you can return to the issue of three and six and ask the child to count upwards, with a big emphasis on three and six, thus:

   One, two, THREE, four, five, SIX.

Day 3.

1. Repeat points 3 and 4 from yesterday.

2. If this is not successful revise yesterday's work. Otherwise move on.

3. If it is successful lay out 5 counters in one pile and 7 counters in another. Ask the child to count each pile and write the number on a piece of paper next to the card. As the child writes each number the child should say the number.

4. Ask the child to pile up the five counters and the seven counters, so that the piles are close together and it is clear that the seven pile is higher than the five pile.

5. Ask the child which number is higher – five or seven. There should now be two reasons for knowing the answer. You pass through five on the way to counting seven, and the seven pile is higher. So the child should say "seven is higher than five".

6. Repeat points 4 and 5 using other numbers such as four and eight, five and nine.

7. Include a couple of examples in which one of the numbers is zero. The child must see there are no counters, write "0" on the card, and say "none".

Day 4.

1. Repeat points 4 and 5 from yesterday.

2. Repeat these again, but this time asking the child which number is lower.

3. Use various pairs of numbers, including the occasional use of zero, to ensure that the child understands "lower".

4. Mix up the questions so that sometimes the child is asked which number is higher and sometimes which number is lower.

Day 5

1. Put nine red counters on the table, and ask the child how many are present.

2. Put down one more counter and ask the child for the number of counters on the table.

3. Continue in this way up to 20. If the child is unsure, remind the child of the number you got to before – as in, "We had fourteen on the table. Here is one more – what number do we have now?" If the child really doesn't know, say the answer. Then go back to the last number that was right, and again add one.

Day 6.

1. Put 19 red counters on the table and ask the child how many there are. Add one more. Ask the child for the answer, if the child does not know, tell the child, write down 20 and ask the child to say the name and copy the number.

2. Put out one blue counter and tell the child it means 10. The child points to it and says "ten" and writes down "10".

3. Put down a second blue counter and tell the child that is "twenty". The child says "twenty", writes down "20" and points to the two blues.

4. Add a third blue counter, and proceed in the same way.

5. Now revise the numbers, checking the child knows 10, 20 and 30. When you are sure there is no misunderstanding here continue up to 90.

Day 7.

1. Place nine blue counters on the table and ask the child what they represent, with the child writing and saying the answer in the normal way.

2. Add one more blue counter and ask what the number is now. If the child does not know, introduce the idea of 100, ask the child to repeat this and write down the number.

3. Put down a green counter and tell the child this is 100. Again the child must repeat and write down 100.

4. Put down two green counters and ask the child what this means. The child should be able to work out that this is 200, and again this is said and written down.

5. Put down one red counter and ask the child to say and write down what it stands for.

6. Repeat point 5 with one blue counter and one green counter.

Day 8.

1. Place nine green counters on the table and ask the child what they represent, with the child writing and saying the answer in the normal way.

2. Add one more green counter and ask what the number is now. If the child does not know, introduce the idea of 1000, ask the child to repeat this and ask the child to write down the number.

3. Put down a yellow counter and tell the child this is 1000. Again the child must repeat and write down 1000.

4. Put down two yellow counters and ask the child what this means. The child should be able to work out that this is 2000, and again this is said and written down.

5. Put down one red counter and ask the child to say and write down what it stands for.

6. Repeat point 5 with one blue counter (10) and then one green counter (100) and finally one yellow counter (1000).

Day 9.

1. Repeat points 5 and 6 from yesterday.

2. Put down a variety of numbers of counters, but only ever use one colour at a time. For example, you might put down three yellow counters (3000), then four blue counters (40), then five red counters (5). The child should say and write down each number.

3. If the child becomes confused between the meanings of red, blue, green and yellow, have the child write out a chart in which the four colours are laid out and next to each is written the appropriate number – 1, 10, 100, 1000.

Part B: Sequencing numbers

Even if a child has a concept of number, that concept cannot be used unless the child also has a firm grasp of the concept of sequencing.

Day 1.

1. Ask the child to write out the numbers 0 to 9 on a set of cards, with one number on each card. If you do not have individual cards, write them on paper, but make the numbers large because the next step is to ask the child to cut these numbers out.

2. Put the child's cut out numbers on the table and ask the child to mix them up. The child then has to put them into the right order, starting with zero and going up to 9.

3. If the child has any problem with this activity, repeat it, and re-run it every day until the child can do it quickly. Time the child and make the timing a game.

4. When the child can work quickly on this sequence, cut out another set of numbers, running from 10 to 19 and combine these with the other numbers and set them out as before, from 0 to 19.

Day 2.

When the child is regularly able to get the sequencing of numbers 0 to 19 correct, move on to the concept of even numbers.

1. Give the child a coin. Ask the child how many sides a coin has. Ignoring the rim (!) the answer is of course two.

2. Put two coins on the table. How many sides do two coins have?

3. Continue with three and four coins – you have now got four answers – 2, 4, 6, 8.

4. Ask the child to select these four numbers from the cut out or card numbers used earlier. If you have been using the numbers a lot you may need to cut out some more numbers. Again, if you can use ready-made 3 x 2 inch cards, so much the better.

5. Ask the child to say with you, "Two, four, six, eight" and point at the numbers as you do so.

6. If the child stumbles or cannot remember this sequence, suggest the child makes up a rhyme – such as:

   Two four six eight
   It's time to go or I'll be late

   The exact words you use don't matter – as long as they help the child to remember the sequence.

7. Ask the child to write down the sequence as 2, 4, 6, 8 and say each number aloud as it is written.

Day 3.

1. Revise point 7 from yesterday.

2. Ask the child to continue the sequence by one more place. The aim is to get the child to work out what comes next – either by counting on two, or going back to the coins, or indeed by any other method.

3. Ask the child to write and say, "2, 4, 6, 8, 10". If it helps, work out a rhyme for this sequence, such as "Two, four, six, eight, ten, go to school then home again." Some children make up really bizarre rhymes – it doesn't matter how silly the rhyme is as long as the child can remember the rhyme and it helps the child remember the sequence.

4. Tell the child this sequence is known as "even numbers". Ask the child to say and write the even numbers up to 10 – the aim is to get the answer "2, 4, 6, 8, 10".

Day 4.

1. Revise point 4 from yesterday.

2. Continue the sequence up to 20.

3. The child should notice that the last numbers in the sequence repeat themselves. Ask the child to arrange the numbers so that 2, 4, 6, 8, 10 are in a line, and 12, 14, 16, 18, 20 are underneath, thus showing that the 2 is over the 12, 4 is over 14 and so on.

4. Now ask the child what number would turn up at the start of the next line. What you are trying to do is get a sequence that looks like this:

2	4	6	8	10
12	14	16	18	20
22	24	26	28	30

5. The point of the exercise is that the child sees that there is a pattern - a sequence - here. The child should see that once you have learned the first group of even numbers, the rest is easy. Even if the child cannot recite the sequence she or he can write the pattern down and then say the sequence.

6. If there is any problem with this, ask the child to make large cut out numbers up to 30 and arrange them in the pattern above.

7. Ask the child to say the even numbers from 2 to 30. The child can look at the chart if he or she wishes.

Day 5.

1. Ask the child to lay out the numbers from 1 to 9.

2. Ask the child to ***remove*** the even numbers.

3. Ask the child to read and say the remaining numbers.

4. Tell the child that these are the odd numbers. Ask the child to recite the odd numbers from 1 to 9 and write them down. Add a rhyme if this helps...

   One, three,
   Five, seven, nine
   Add the numbers
   In a line

Day 6.

1. Ask the child to set out the odd numbers and recite them. Set the numbers out in a sequence across the table:

   1 3 5 7 9

2. Now place the number 11 under the number 1, and say the next number in the sequence is 11. Do the same with 13. The table will now look like this:

1	3	5	7	9
11	13			

3. Ask the child what comes next. The child has to find the number 15 and place it under the 5, and then do the same with 17 and 19.

4. Ask the child to say the odd number sequence from 1 to 19.

Day 7.

1. Ask the child to set out and say the odd sequence from 1 to 19.

2. Ask the child to set out and say the even sequence from 2 to 30.

3. Ask the child to clear away the odd number sequence, and lay it out again up to 29, using the pattern already established. If the child has any problem with this, re-work the odd number sequence as established so far and talk with the child about where the sequence will lead next.

4. Ask the child to clear away the even number sequence, and now write it and say it up to 50, using the same approach as before.

Day 8.

1. Repeat part 4 of yesterday's work using card cut out numbers or number cards the child has made himself/herself.

2. Ask the child to pick out or circle every number that ends in "0" (e.g. 10, 20 etc)

3. Ask the child to pick out or circle every number that ends in "5" (e.g. 5, 15, etc)

4. Ask the child to gather together all the numbers selected in parts 2 and 3 above and put them in numerical order showing the pattern of 0 and 5 numbers, like this:

5	10
15	20

5. Ask the child to say and write down the numbers. Ask the child what he/she knows about this sequence. The answer could be that all the numbers are 5 apart, or that they all end in 5 or 0, or that the numbers ending in 5 or 0 alternate. All three answers are correct.

6. Show the child the number square below and ask the child to find sequences of numbers that end in 0 and 5 alternately. (The answer is that the sequence appears twice, once horizontally and once vertically.)

Number square

	0	**1**	**2**	**3**	**4**	**5**	**6**	**7**	**8**	**9**	**10**
0	0	0	0	0	0	0	0	0	0	0	0
1	0	1	2	3	4	5	6	7	8	9	10
2	0	2	4	6	8	10	12	14	16	18	20
3	0	3	6	9	12	15	18	21	24	27	30
4	0	4	8	12	16	20	24	28	32	36	40
5	0	5	10	15	20	25	30	35	40	45	50
6	0	6	12	18	24	30	36	42	48	54	60
7	0	7	14	21	28	35	42	49	56	63	70
8	0	8	16	24	32	40	48	56	64	72	80
9	0	9	18	27	36	45	54	63	72	81	90
10	0	10	20	30	40	50	60	70	80	90	100

Day 9.

1. Ask the child to draw a number square grid and to write in just the sequences that end in 0 and 5.

2. Ask the child to find the lines that consist of **all** the odd and even numbers (up to 10), and write those in (you might need to explain to the child that these are the lines with the numbers 1, 2, 3, 4 etc). These two lines are the 1 times table, but there is no need to point this out at this moment.

3. Ask the child to find the lines that only include even numbers and to write those in (the 2, 4, 6, 8, and 10 times tables lines). This is the first statement that multiples of even numbers are always even numbers. Put another way, there is no odd number in the 2 times table no matter how high you go. The same is true of all even tables. If the child is fascinated by the pattern, then explore this issue as far as the child wishes to take it.

Day 10.

1. Ask the child to lay out cards for the "9" line in the number grid – 9, 18, 27 etc.

2. Ask the child to look at these numbers and see if he/she notices anything about them. The answer we are looking for here is that the first number of each pair goes up and the second number comes down in the sequence. The key point that the child should become aware of is that there is some sort of pattern here. We are not asking the child to learn his/her 9 times table, but rather to understand the notion of the numbers moving in sequence.

3. Ask the child if 9 is an odd number or an even number. If the child can't remember, go back to the coins (Day 2 of sequencing) – if the number is equal to the number of sides on some coins then it is an even number. So one coin has two sides, two coins have four sides, and so on. The child can write this down, or use the number chart, and see if 9 occurs. It does not and so 9 is not an even number – it is an odd number.

Day 11.

1. Ask the child to look at the completed number chart. Ask the child to track across the line for the number "8". Can the child see any sequences, or anything that makes a pattern? The answers could be that all the numbers are even, or that the second numbers descend in twos (8, 6, 4, 2). If the child does not come up with any ideas point the child towards the answer and keep giving hints until she or he gets there. Then return to the theme tomorrow.

2. Ask the child to create a sequence of numbers which have something in common. The child might come up with a list of even numbers, or an ascending sequence of numbers, or a times table taken from the number chart – any answer is fine as long as there is something that holds the numbers together. If the child can't come up with any sequence, take the child back to the number chart and ask the child to look again for a sequence.

Day 12.

1. Ask the child to write and say the numbers from 0 to 10 in ascending order. You may well have to explain ***ascending***. If this is a new word for the child, make sure the child can say it back to you as she or he is preparing to write the numbers.

2. Ask the child to write and say the numbers from 10 to 0 in descending order. If there is any confusion between ascending and descending, the child might be helped by remembering that 'descending' and 'down' both start with the same letter and the same sound.

3. If these two exercises have gone without a hitch ask the child to repeat them but this time using the numbers from 10 to 20. If there is a problem, do not move on, but revise ascending and descending, and then return to points 1 and 2 tomorrow. When they are securely learned the section is completed.

Activity 1

- Lay out a range of items on the table. These can be pens, pencils, cards, etc at school, cups, saucers, fruit, knives, etc at home.

- Ask the child to take a look at the objects.

- Ask the child to look away, or close his/her eyes.

- Remove one or two items.

- Ask the child if there are more or less items.

Irrespective of how well the child performed in this task, ask the child how she/he got to the answer. We need to compare two pieces of information here – did the child get the answer right or wrong, and did the child count the number of items.

If the child got the answer right and counted the total before and after, no corrective action is required and you can repeat the game by adding or taking away more items.

If the child got the answer right but did not count, but instead had a feel for the number, or remembered all the objects, repeat the activity with more and more items. If the child can continue to get the answer right then do not force the child to count, but note that this child has an internal estimating system.

If the child got the answer wrong and counted, give the child extra help in counting various objects. Keep changing the objects so that the child gets the idea that the nature of the objects does not affect the mathematics.

If the child got the answer wrong and did not count, suggest to the child that counting before and after can be a helpful approach.

Activity 2

Two or more people play "I went to market" with numbers.

> *The first says, "I went to the market and I bought one apple"*
> *The second says, "I went to the market and I bought two apples."*
> *The third (or first if only two players) says, "I went to the market and I bought three apples"*

And so on up to 10. Then the process works backwards down the numbers.

Next the game is played with two items

> *"I went to market and I bought one apple and two oranges"*
> *"I went to market and I bought two apples and three oranges"*
> *"I went to market and I bought three apples and four oranges"*

and so on.

You can make the game as difficult as you wish – but don't do this until you have tried the easier versions first. Find out where the child starts making mistakes, and do not press on beyond that point until the child can play the game on a slightly easier level.

Activity 3

Ask the child to get out some objects and put them on the table.... For example:

> *"Get me four pencils."*
>
> *"Now get me some knives – I want more knives than pencils."*
>
> *"Now get me some pens. I want fewer pens than knives."*

And so on.

Section 2: Multi-sensory addition

Day 1.

For this section you will use Table 1 – see page 33.

1. Take ten red counters and set them on the table. The child does not have to count them, or recognise that there are ten on the table.

2. Select five red counters and move them away from the original group, and ask the child how many counters you have selected.

3. The way in which the child answers is important, and the technique explained here is used throughout these multi-sensory addition activities. The child touches the counters, counting them out if necessary, then says the answer "five" and finally writes the number 5 in the first column in Table 1. If the child has difficulty with this, for example if the child cannot remember what "5" looks like, take a card and write "5" on it, and place five red counters by it. Ask the child to do the exercise again. If it helps, let the child copy a "5" that you have written down. If there is a problem, repeat this with other numbers until the child can see any number of counters up to 9, say the number, and write down the figure. If there is no problem the child should write down "5" in the first column of Table 1.

4. Start again, and create a pile of two red counters from the original group of ten. Ask the child "how many counters are there here now?" The child touches the newly formed group of two, counts them up if necessary, and says "two" and writes in the number 2 in the middle column, next to the 5 in the left hand column.

5. You now set out a pile of five counters and a pile of two counters, moving the remaining counters to one side. The child points to the five red counters and then the number 5 in the first column and says "five". This is then repeated for the pile of two counters.

6. Now push the two piles together, and ask the child how many counters there are now. If the child can immediately say "seven" and does not need to count, then you might be undertaking work that is too easy for the child. There is no benefit in going over work that the child already knows – she or he will soon get bored, and nothing will have been achieved. Try two more questions – if again the answer is given at once, move on to Day 2.

7. Continuing to work with red counters, work on other sums which have answers up to ten counters and writing the answers in Table 1.

Day 2.

For this activity you will use Table 2 – see page 34.

1. Revise point 7 from yesterday by undertaking two questions. If the child makes a mistake, continue to work with this activity until the child gets them all right. If this continues for over 5 minutes stop the activity, and come back to it tomorrow. Don't proceed until the child can do this work correctly.

2. When you know that the child is perfectly happy with this operation move on to using Table 2. The activity with the second table is just the same as yesterday's work, except that you and the child must now also use the words "plus" and "equals". Please make sure you stick with these words and that you don't use any variants, such as "add". "Add" is a perfectly adequate word, but many children get confused between the various ways of saying "plus" ("add", "sum of", "and") and so it is better to stick to one word. (If your child is at a school that always uses "add" then obviously you can change to "add" throughout and not use "plus").

3. The activity in Table 2 also requires that the child writes in + and = in the columns shown. Thus the child will be writing down

$$4 + 3 = 7$$

   in the relevant columns. Each time the child writes "+" the child must say "plus" and each time the child writes "=" the child says "equals". (Again do not combine the use of "equals" with the use of "makes" or "is". Always stick to the same word.)

4. Choose some more sums. Which sums you choose do not matter at this stage providing the total of the two numbers is always under 10.

5. Now extend the exercise by adding the concept of nought. Put out five red counters on one side of the table, and next to them place a card with "0" on it with no red counters. The child must say and write

$$5 + 0 = 5$$

   You must decide what you are going to call "0" – and again you should stick to one word. Most children call it "nought" but you can also use "zero" if the child is happier with that. "Nothing" is not normally considered to be a mathematical word, and should be avoided unless the child makes a particular fuss about wanting that word.

Day 3.

For this activity you will use Table 3 – see page 35.

1. Once the child is happy with the sums which add up to less than 10, and with the concept of 0, it is time to increase the range of numbers with sums that add up to 18 or less, using the numbers between 0 and 9. Set out the work as yesterday, and use Table 3 for recording the answers.

2. If the child starts to get confused over the counting of the red counters then you can help the child by using the following technique. If you have set the problem of adding 7 + 8 = ___, and the child is simply miscounting on the way to 15, ask the child to count the red counters until he or she gets to 10. Then at this point, pile the 10 counters up and set them to one side. Now go on and count the remaining 5, counting them as eleven, twelve, thirteen, fourteen and fifteen. The child can then say and write down 15.

3. If you think that there might be some confusion here return to the first section of this course on numbers and revise the numbers up to 20.

4. Once you have a technique working satisfactorily, stick to that technique, and keep working on pairs of numbers that are between 0 and 9, with answers up to 18, until the child gets the answer right each time without any hesitation.

Day 4.

For this activity you will use Table 4 – see page 36.

1. Revise the final point of yesterday's work.

2. Now the child is ready to add together numbers in which the answer is to be anything up to 99. To begin, take the usual two piles of red counters, and make them up to 11 and 12 counters. Don't tell the child that you have 11 and 12 counters, but rather tell the child that he or she has to work out the totals.

3. The first thing the child has to do is to count the totals and, in order to remember the numbers, say the totals and write them down as numerals. In addition the child should separate out the ten, and put that pile on a place setting marked:

   Ten
   10

4. Now it should be clear to the child that there are eleven (a pile of ten, and a one) and twelve (a pile of ten and two) counters. If it is not clear, the work from the last two days needs to be revised.

5. But before we go on to add these numbers up, it is worth commenting to the child that this is getting a bit difficult to manage. And we are running out of red counters. Is it possible to represent ten red counters in another way? Ask for suggestions.

6. The child may well come up with the idea of having one blue counter representing ten red counters. If not, try to guide the child in this direction. And if the child suggests a banana instead of a blue counter, accept the banana – if you have one. Indeed the children who come up with the really odd ideas are the ones who often make the fastest progress here. The fact is that "blue counter = 10" is the sensible answer, but "battered car from the game last played 2 years ago = 10" is much more likely to stay in the memory.

7. Assuming for the sake of simplicity, that we settle on blue counters meaning 10, the child is now faced with a blue counter and a red counter, meaning eleven.

8. Show the child the blue and red counter and ask what number they represent together. If the child slips on this, remind the child of the meaning of the blue counter. When the child says eleven the child should also write down 11 in Table four.

Day 5.

1. Repeat point 8 from yesterday.

2. Now repeat this point with the blue counter and two reds. If the child is still stumbling over the meaning of the blue counter, forget the sum, and go back to ten red counters, and how to represent them. Stay with that point until it is secure. The child should physically count the ten red counters, write down 10, and then put down

the blue counter and remove the red counters, saying "the blue counter is 10, so I don't need the ten red counters!"

3. When you think the child is secure with the concept of the ten being equal to one blue counter, go back to the 11 + 12 problem and see if the child can quote the numbers involved, pointing to the one blue and one red and saying "ten plus one equals eleven". (Remember we are sticking to the words "plus" and "equals" in all these sums).

4. Now proceed to the issue of adding these two (11 + 12) together. Ask the child how to do it – it is worth allowing the child to try and work out his/her own strategy because if the child can work out his or her own approach then it is most likely to be a solution that is going to stick.

5. If the child gets the answer right using an invented strategy move on to another problem – for example 12 + 13. If the strategy works each time that is fine.

6. If the child does not get anywhere suggest that he/she tries combining the blue counters to make 2 blue counters. Ask the child what 2 blue counters represents. The child should see that this represents the number 20. Then suggest that the child combines the red counters – that should bring the answer 3 and should enable the child to see that the answer is 23. If the child shows any uncertainty at this point help him/her to convert back to red counters and prove the answer by counting them out.

Day 6.

1. Lay out the numbers 12 and 11 using blue and red counters.

2. Ask the child what those numbers are. As always the child should touch, write down and say the numbers.

3. Ask the child to add them up and to say and write down the total.

4. Repeat the activity with other pairs of numbers.

5. Once the child is clearly getting these sums right, ask the child to do one more thing: ask the child to write in the answers in a conventional sum that looks like this:

$$\begin{array}{r} 11 \\ +12 \\ \hline \\ \hline \end{array}$$

6. If the child gets this wrong, go back to the previous stage and set out 11 and 12 using the red and blue counters and then return to the written version. If the child gets the answer right, move on. In either case, insist that the child writes out the numbers as set out above, and insist that the child says each number as she or he writes it. Do remember that the child can be getting the answer right, even if the child is starting by adding 1+1, and then adds 1+2. We know that this will lead to false answers when the numbers in the units column on the right add up to over 9. But the child does not know this. Allow the child to continue in this way for the time being. Remember that information that is discovered is always more likely to be remembered than information which is given as instruction.

7. Repeat activity 5 by adding 12 and 12, 11 and 13 and so on, until the time for the day is up, but do not use any number over 14.

Day 7.

1. Repeat three sums from day 6. Only continue if the child is secure in his/her knowledge of this work. Otherwise go back and revise.

2. Put out two blue counters. Ask the child what each counter means (each means 10). Now ask the child to add them together by writing the numbers down with the + sign between them. If the child does not know "20" and "twenty" as the answer, tell the child. Ask the child to repeat the operation by putting the two blues together and saying the sum as he/she does so. Then change one of the blue counters to a pile of 10 red counters, to check that the child knows that the blue 10 is the same as the ten individual red counters. Then change the second blue counter to a pile of ten reds, and repeat the sum. Finally go back to two blues, which should be added to make 20, using the counters, words and symbols.

3. Put out three blue counters, and establish that the three can be added together to make 30. If this is not clear to the child, return to point 2 above, revise the making of 20, and then add in the third blue, and proceed as before, changing the blue to 10 reds on occasion.

4. Now set out the red and blue counters to represent 15 and 16. Ask the child what each number is, and ask the child to write the numbers down and say them.

5. Ask the child to add 15 and 16 using the counters and if the child wishes, using a pen and paper. Observe the process carefully. If the child gets the answer right, move on to adding 16 + 17, 16 + 16 and finally 15 + 18 and then stop. Watch to see if the process is the same each time. If it is, and the answer is correct each time, you should not change the child's system even if it appears wrong, confused, or overly long or unnecessarily complex.

6. In adding up 15 and 16 using red and blue counters the child will get to a position of having 11 red counters and 2 blue counters. Ask the child if there is anything we can do to cut out the number of red counters. How else can we write 11, except with 11 red counters?

7. If the child is having problems with any of these questions ask the child to work with you, explaining the system he/she is using step by step. If we take 15 and 16 the child might put the two blue counters together. Does the child know this is 20? If not, this is once again the area to focus on. Put down one blue, and then another and ask for the answer of what two blues make. If there is a consistent problem return to the section of this book on numbers before going any further.

Day 8.

1. Ask the child to copy down the sum:

```
 15
+16
___

___
```

If the child gets it right, move on to other sums involving combinations of 15, 16, 17, 18 and 19.

2. If the child has problems ask the child to take you through the method she/he is using here. A typical problem involves the child adding the two tens first, and so getting to this point:

```
 15
+16
___
2
___
```

In this case the problem of adding the 5 and 6 occurs. The child might make this 11 but simply write in a 1, or might write in the "11" to give an answer such as

```
 15
+16
___
211
___
```

3. Do not rush to tell the child to work from right to left – this will just seem meaningless to the child and is the sort of arbitrary rule that may have caused the child problems in the past. Remember this is a real live problem that the child has to solve.

4. Return to the multi-sensory approach adding a blue and five red counters to a blue and six red counters. If the child can do that and get the right answer, point out to the child that this answer is right – the answer works like this:

- 1 blue and 5 red + 1 blue and 6 red = 2 blues and 11 reds
- 11 reds = 1 blue and 1 red.
- So we now have 2 blues and 1 blue and 1 red
- 2 blues, and 1 blue and 1 red = 3 blues and 1 red
- 3 blues and 1 red = 31
- Now try point 2 (above) again.

Day 9.

1. We can take 15 + 16 in two ways. Using the multi-sensory approach the child should be able to resolve this into 3 blue and 1 red, making 31. So we now know that:

```
 15
+16
___
 31
___
```

2. How can this be? Write this sum out and ask the child to work on this problem in a way that produces the right answer. If there is no progress at all, you can now say, "what is 5 + 6?" and get the answer "11". That should provide a clue – that it is the right numbers that can be added first. But remember the idea here is that the child works out a way of adding up the numbers to get what the red and blue counters reveal to be the right answer.

3. One resolution of the difficulty we see sometimes is this:

```
15
16
__
2
11
__
31
```

Here the left column is added up to get "2", and then the right column is added up to get 11 which is written under the 2 and then the totals are added.

An alternative approach looks like this:

```
15
16
__
11
__
31
```

What the child is doing is working out the right column first and getting 11, and then writing that in as an answer. Then the child works out the left column, which now has the extra one.

This is virtually the traditional method of "carrying one" but for the dyscalculic child it is a much better model, because it avoids what is essentially the mumbo-jumbo of "carry one" or any variation on that theme.

Some teachers don't like this version because they state that there is a danger that the child will go back and add up the right column again – but one can counter this by saying that every method has its problems. The fact is that if the child has devised his or her own method and can proudly show that method off to parents and teachers, the child is much more likely to remember it as "my method" rather than remember a method that is forced on him or her.

Day 10.

1. Having reached a conclusion that works, now return to the other questions involving 15, 16, 17, 18, 19 and ask the child to work the questions both ways - once with the counters and once with the devised mathematical system - and to check that the answer really comes out the same each time. Also make sure the child is working on the same system each time - having devised a system the child should stay with it. If

the child swaps systems, ask the child why, and try to get the child to adopt his or her "best" system.

Day 11.

1. With the child fully secure with addition using numbers up to 19, move on to addition using numbers up to 24, firstly using red and blue counters, and then checking the answer with the symbolic representation.

2. Do not proceed if the child is getting sums wrong – always go back to a previous point and ensure that the process has been fully understood, and then move forward again.

3. If the child is getting the sums right, continue with larger numbers, and totals up to 99.

Day 12.

1. Put down 9 red counters and ask the child to say the number. Then add one more red counter. The child should say "ten" and write down "10". Ask the child to change the 10 red counters to something that is easier to see – the child should remove the 10 red counters and replace with a blue counter.

2. Put down 9 blue counters and ask the child to say the number. Then add one more blue counter. The child should say "one hundred" and write down "100". Ask the child to change the 10 blue counters to something that is easier to see – we will assume that the child will remove the 10 blue counters and replace with a green counter.

3. Put down 6 green counters and ask the child what that represents. The child should be able to say and write 600. If the child has a problem here, take the child back over point 2, and then keep adding one more green counter.

4. Ask the child to add 50 + 50 using counters and then with the sum as written below:

$$\begin{array}{r} 50 \\ +50 \\ \hline \\ \hline \end{array}$$

Day 13.

1. Ask the child to add 52 + 53 using counters and the mathematical representation:

$$\begin{array}{r} 52 \\ +53 \\ \hline \\ \hline \end{array}$$

2. The child should be able to get this sum correct now. If so also work on 53 + 54 and 52 + 25.

3. Now move on to 55 + 56. Following the approach used earlier you have to encourage the child to develop his or her own mathematical approach which gives the same answer as the multi-sensory approach. If the child tries to cheat and just write down the multi-sensory answer in the mathematical representation, ask the child to show you how she or he is working. If the child cannot (and there are many dyscalculic children who cannot) do another mathematical question, without doing the multi-sensory work first, and use the answer the child gets to see if the child is indeed working in a meaningful way which the child understands.

Day 14.

1. Ask the child to add 63 + 64 and 72 + 75 using both systems.

2. If the child can do these sums correctly, move on to 65 + 68. This is the first sum that involves answers in **both** mathematical columns which exceed 9. The multi-sensory approach should lead to this type of resolution:

   - Six blue and five red, plus six blue and eight red, equals
   - Twelve blue and five red and eight red, equals
   - Twelve blue and 13 red, equals
   - One green and two blue and 13 red, equals
   - One green and two blue and one blue and three red, equals
   - One green and three blue and three red, equals
   - 133

3. Now try 88 + 39; 60 + 99; 55 + 66.

4. If the child is having problems return to this day's work tomorrow. If not continue with day 15 tomorrow.

Day 15.

1. Ask the child to set out in counters the number "two hundred and thirty four". The child should also be able to write the number down and say it. If there is a problem remind the child of the meaning of red, blue and green counters.

2. Ask the child to add up 123 + 234 using first the multi-sensory method, and then using the mathematical representation.

3. If all is working well, ask the child to add 128 + 237. This should remind the child of how to deal with totals greater than 9. Again make sure the child works both in a multi-sensory way, and using mathematical representation.

4. Once the child has confidence in adding sums where the units add up to more than 9, move to a sum in which the tens column adds up to more than 99 – for example, 162 + 373.

Day 16.

1. The child should be using the same system to accommodate units above 9, and tens above 99. Revise the final step of yesterday's work and now ask the child to add 378 + 278. In this case the child has got to handle an overload in both the first two columns. Watch the working carefully to make sure it is consistent.

2. Put down 9 blue counters and ask the child to say the number. Then add one more blue counter. The child should say "one hundred" and write down "100". Ask the child to change the 10 blue counters to something that is easier to see – we will assume that the child will remove the 10 blue counters and replace them with a green counter.

3. Put down 9 green counters and ask the child what that represents. The child should be able to say and write 900.

4. Put down 1 more green counter and ask the child what the total is. If the child is not sure about "one thousand" and "1000" help the child by putting down one red, and asking the child to write "1" next to it, one blue with "10" next to it, one green with "100" next to it, and then finally one yellow, and write "1000" next to it. As each number is written it should be spoken.

5. Ask the child to add 500 + 500 using counters and then with the sum as written below:

```
 500
+500
____

____
```

Day 17.

1. Ask the child to set out in counters the number "two thousand one hundred and forty four". The child should also be able to write the number down and say it. If there is a problem remind the child of the meaning of red, blue, green and yellow counters.

2. Ask the child to add up 1123 + 1234 using first the multi-sensory method, and then using the mathematical representation.

3. If all is working well, ask the child to add 2128 + 3237. This should remind the child of how to deal with totals greater than 9. Again make sure the child works both in a multi-sensory way, and using mathematical representation.

4. Once the child has confidence in adding sums where the units add up to more than 9, move to a sum in which the tens column adds up to more than 99 – for example, 2162 + 3373.

5. Now ask the child to add up 3662 + 4701, using both systems.

Day 18.

1. Repeat point 5 above. If the answer is correct using both systems, ask the child to add up 6220 + 6301. Ask the child to say the answer – there should not be a new coloured counter to represent ten thousand, since we don't have a separate word for "ten thousand" in the way that we have "thousand" meaning "ten hundred".

2. If this sum is undertaken correctly, move on to the final set of sums:

   - 6309 + 7988 =
   - 8543 + 8373 =
   - 9099 + 3456 =

   If the child can do these three, then the child can handle addition. The methodology used might still not be what you would like to see, and it might not be elegant, but it works and gives the right answer.

   If you wish, you can suggest what you consider to be a simpler method of adding up using mathematical representation. Some children react against such ideas, some welcome them. If you get a reaction against, leave the issue. After all, great progress has been made. The child can add numbers up to 99,999.

Activity 4

- Ask the child to tell you the name of all the wooden things in the room.
- Ask him/her how many such items there are. Don't write the number down – remember it and see if the child does also.
- Ask the child to tell you the name of all the plastic (or metal, or indeed any other defining characteristic) items in the room.
- Again ask her/him how many such items there are. Again, there should be no writing down of the number.
- Ask the child how many wooden and metal items there are in the room. This is obviously a simple addition.

If the child gets this right, repeat the exercise with questions that will lead to larger numbers. If the child always gets the answer right with no attempt to write the number down, then you may note that the child has a very developed sense of mental arithmetic

If the child gets the sum wrong ask the child the method being used. If the child is counting and adding, suggest to the child that he or she writes the totals down as they go along if this is not being done. If this is being done and the totals are still wrong, go through the process with the child step by step to find the problem. Then play the game each day until the child can get the right answer.

Activity 5

- Ask the child to draw a picture of two cars – or bring in a picture with two or more cars in it. Highlight two cars.
- Ask the child how many wheels each car has – including wheels that cannot be seen in the picture.
- Ask how many wheels there are on two cars.

- If the child gets the answer right, try with two cars and a motorcycle.

Activity 6

- Ask the child how many people there are in a room. The answer should be 30 or more. You can do this using a real room with pupils in it, or a picture. The picture can be drawn using stick men, to save time.

- Once you have the answer ask the child how she or he got the answer. If the child has a method that always works, and is not unduly cumbersome, do not try to change the method. If the child does not get the answer right, or has a method that takes a very long time to give an answer, suggest a new method to the child. You can suggest that the child groups the people into smaller groups – for example 10s. So the child might end up with three groups of 10, plus one left over. The child then has to add 10 + 10 + 10 to get 30 and then the one left over to get 31.

- Questions of this type can be extended if the child enjoys them, for example by using pictures and asking, "how many legs and how many dogs are there in this picture" etc. Questions can be adjusted to suit the pictures you have available.

Table 1

First number	Second number	Total

Table 2

First number	+	Second number	=	Total

Table 3

First number	+	Second number	=	Total

Table 4

First number	+	Second number	=	Total

Section 3: Multi-sensory subtraction

Day 1.

For this activity you will use Table 5 – see page 47.

1. Take ten red counters and set them on the table. The child does not have to count them, or recognise that there are ten on the table.

2. Select five red counters and move them away from the original group. Ask the child how many counters you have selected.

3. The way in which the child answers is important, and the technique explained here is used throughout these multi-sensory subtraction activities. The child touches the counters, counting them out if necessary, and then says the answer "five" and writes the number 5 in the first column in Table 5. If the child has difficulty with this – for example if the child cannot remember what "5" looks like - take a piece of paper and ask the child to do the exercise again. If it helps, let the child copy a "5" that you have written down. Repeat this with other numbers until the child can see any number of counters up to 9, say the number, and write down the figure.

4. Now remove three red counters from the group of five. Put them a little to the right of the remaining group of two counters. Ask the child "how many counters did I take away?" The child touches the three that have been removed, says "three" and writes in the number 3 in the middle column, next to the 5 in the left hand column.

5. You now push the three counters away, leaving just two counters in the centre of the table, and ask how many counters there are left. The child counts them, and says "two" and writes in the number 2 in the final column. (If the child can immediately say "two" and does not need to count, then you might be undertaking work that is too easy for the child. There is no benefit in going over work that the child already knows – she or he will soon get bored, and nothing will have been achieved. Try two more questions – if again the answer is given at once, move on to Day 2.)

6. Continuing to work only with red counters, work on other sums which start with up to 10 red counters and take some away.

Day 2.

For this activity you will use Table 6 – see page 48.

1. Revise point 6 from yesterday by undertaking two questions. If the child makes a mistake, continue to work on this activity until the child gets them all right. If this continues for over 5 minutes stop the activity and come back to it tomorrow. Don't proceed until the child can do this work correctly.

2. When you know that the child is perfectly happy with this operation move on to using Table 6. The activity with the second table is just the same as yesterday's work, except that you and the child must now also use the words "take away" and "equals". Please make sure you stick with these words and that you don't use any variants, such as "minus". "Minus" is a perfectly adequate word, but many children

get confused between the various ways of saying "take away" ("minus", "less", "remove", "subtract") and so it is better to stick to one word. (If your child is at a school that always uses "minus" then obviously you can change to "minus" throughout and not use "take away".)

The activity in Table 6 also requires that the child writes in "–" and "=" in the columns shown. Thus the child will be writing down:

$$4 - 3 \ = 1$$

in the relevant columns. Each time the child writes "–" the child must say "take away" and each time the child writes "=" the child says "equals". (Again do not combine the use of "equals" with the use of "makes" or "is". Always stick to the same word.)

3. Choose some more sums. Which sums you choose do not matter at this stage providing the numbers you start with are all under 10.

4. Now extend the exercise by adding the concept of nought. Put out five red counters and then remove five. The child must say and write:

$$5 - 5 = 0$$

You must decide what you are going to call "0" – and again you should stick to one word. Most children call it "nought" but you can also use "zero" if the child is happier with that. "Nothing" is not normally considered to be a mathematical word, and should be avoided unless the child makes a particular fuss about wanting that word.

Day 3.

For this activity you will use Table 7 – see page 49.

1. Once the child is happy with the subtractions using numbers under 10, and with the concept of 0, it is time to increase the range of numbers up to 19. Set out the work as yesterday, and use Table 7 for recording the answers.

2. If the child starts to get confused over the counting of the red counters then you can help the child by using the following technique. If you have set the problem 15 – 8 = ____, and the child is simply miscounting on the way to 15, ask the child to count the red counters until he or she gets to 10. Then at this point, pile the 10 counters up and set them to one side. Now go on and count the remaining 5, counting them as eleven, twelve, thirteen, fourteen and fifteen. The child can then write down 15.

3. If you believe there might be confusion here return to the first section of this course on numbers and revise the numbers up to 20.

4. Once you have a technique working satisfactorily, stick to that technique, and keep working on pairs of numbers that are between 1 and 19 until the child gets the answer right each time without any hesitation.

Day 4.

1. Revise the final point of yesterday's work.

2. Now the child is ready to undertake subtractions with numbers from 1 to 99, where the answer is positive. To begin, take the usual pile of red counters, this time doing the calculation 14 – 9 = ___. Don't tell the child that you have set out 14 counters, but rather tell the child that he or she has to work out the total.

3. The first thing the child has to do is to count the total, and in order to remember the numbers, say the total and write it down as numerals. Also the child should separate out the ten, and put that pile on a place setting marked:

   Ten
   10

4. Now it should be clear to the child that there are fourteen (a pile of ten, and a pile of four) counters and taking away 9 is easy. You can then count the result.

5. Next tell the child we are going to start with 25 counters. But we can see at once that this is getting a bit difficult to manage. And we are running out of red counters. If the child has completed the earlier sections of this book the child should immediately suggest we use blue counters (or whatever other symbol has been agreed) for ten. If you have moved straight to this part of the book you will need to ask the child to come up with a simpler way to represent 25. See **Day 4** in the section on **Addition** for more thoughts on this process.

6. Assuming for the sake of simplicity, that we settle on blue counters meaning 10, the child is now faced with 25 being represented by two blue counters and five red counters.

7. Show the child the blue and red counters and ask what number that means. If the child slips on this, remind the child of the meaning of the blue counter. When the child says 25 the child should also write down 25 in Table 7.

8. Tell the child you want to take away 13 – the child should be able to do this by taking away one blue and three red counters. If not, help the child with suggestions. The child should complete writing the sum in Table 7.

Day 5.

1. Repeat points 6 to 8 from yesterday.

2. If the child is still stumbling over the problem, go back to red counters only, then reintroduce the blue, and try again. Remember the rule here must be that you can only take red from red, and blue from blue.

3. Now try several more subtractions of this type, such as 29 – 18, 22 – 21, 18 – 15, and so on. In each case make sure the questions allow the removal of reds from reds and blues from blues. So at this point we do not ask 12 – 6 as that would lead to a problem. Each time ask the child to write the completed subtraction in Table 7.

4. When you think the child is secure with the concept of subtraction, ask the child again about the relationship between the red counter and the blue counter. The answer should be that ten red counters equal one blue counter.

5. Now put on the table one blue and two red counters to equal 12. Ask the child the number. Now say "take away 6". The only way the child can do this is to change the blue into ten reds (making 12 in all) so that you can now remove 6.

6. Now try other subtractions with the same issue. 14 – 5, 11 – 9, 17 – 8. The child must say the subtraction as he/she does it.

7. If all is working well ask the child to do a mixture of subtractions, some of which need the transfer of the blues into reds, and some of which do not, such as 16 – 8, 17 – 5, 9 – 3, 12 – 4.

Day 6.

1. Lay out the number 15 using one blue and five red counters.

2. Ask the child what the number is. As always the child should touch, write down and say the number.

3. Ask the child to take away 12 and to say and write down the total.

4. Now ask the child to do one more thing: ask the child to write in the answers to a conventional sum that looks like this:

$$\begin{array}{r} 15 \\ -12 \\ \hline \\ \hline \end{array}$$

5. If the child gets this wrong, go back to the previous stage and show the child that the subtraction is the same with the counters as it is with the formal mathematical layout. If the child gets the answer right, move on. In either case, insist that the child writes out the numbers as set out above, and insist that the child says each number as she or he writes it.

6. Now ask the child to copy the subtractions below and do them using the mathematical approach first and then to check by using the multi-sensory approach. If the child cannot do this, ask the child to say the numbers, and work on a strategy together. Several routes are possible – the child can start with the lower number and count up using his/her fingers. So in 12 – 6 the child says "7, 8, 9, 10, 11, 12" ticking off each number on a finger until she/he sees the answer is 6. Or the child can count from 12 backwards. Or the child can count down from 12 to 10, and know at once that is 2. Then the child goes from 10 down to 6, and gets 4. Then the 4 and 2 are added together. It doesn't matter which strategy is used and you should avoid giving the child a strategy – no matter how cumbersome the child's particular approach turns out to be.

14	16	18	12
- 8	- 9	- 9	-6
___	___	___	___
___	___	___	___

Day 7.

1. Repeat three sums from exercise 6 above. Only continue if the child is secure in his/her knowledge of this work. Otherwise go back and revise.

2. Put out two blue counters. Ask the child what each counter means (each means 10, so together they mean 20). Ask the child to do the sum 20 – 10 = ___ and to write it in Table 7. This should be simple as it involves taking 1 blue counter away. Show the child that it can be written:

   20
   -10
   ___
   10
   ___

3. Ask the child to do the sums below and check the answers using the multi-sensory method. He/she should understand that red counters can only be taken from red counters and blue from blue. If he/she is getting these right set some more as practice but ensure that the bottom numbers are all smaller than the top numbers at this stage.

25	36	47	85	143
-13	-24	-31	-52	-31
___	___	___	___	___
___	___	___	___	___

4. Now ask the child to do the sum 31 – 22 using the multi-sensory method. The only way the child can do this is by changing one of the blue counters into 10 red counters. That means he/she now performs the calculation:

   - 3 blue and 1 red counter – 2 blue and 2 red counters =
   - 2 blue and 11 red counters – 2 blue and 2 red counters =
   - 0 blue and 9 red counters
   - The answer is that 31 – 22 = 9.

5. Now ask the child to do a number of subtractions similar to 31 – 22 using the method in 4 above, and ensuring that the highest number used does not go above 99.

Day 8.

1. Repeat exercise 5 from day 7 above to check that the child still remembers the method of working. If not go back and work with the counters until you feel that the child has grasped it.

2. Ask the child to do the following sum and watch closely how he/she does it. If the answer is correct give the child a few more examples to do where the units on the bottom are greater than the units on the top. The child should be comfortable with converting one blue counter into 10 red so that the subtraction can be done.

$$\begin{array}{r} 43 \\ -35 \\ \hline \\ \hline \end{array}$$

3. You can now explain that the workings for this calculation which the child has been doing with counters can be set out in the following way.

$$\begin{array}{r} 43 \\ -35 \\ \hline \\ \hline \end{array} \quad \Longrightarrow \quad \begin{array}{r} 3^{1}3 \\ -3\ 5 \\ \hline 0\ 8 \\ \hline \end{array} \qquad \text{which equals 8.}$$

Explain to the child and demonstrate using counters that the top number $3^{1}3$ is equivalent to 3 blue and 13 red counters:

- The top line of the subtraction is equivalent to 4 blue and 3 red counters.
- The child then transfers 1 blue counter to 10 red counters so that he/she now has 3 blue and 13 red.
- The child can now do the subtraction 3 blue and 13 red – 3 blue and 5 red = 8 red.

This is the traditional method of borrowing and is at its simplest if the child works from the right in the same way as he/she did in the addition section earlier in this book.

Day 9.

1. Revise the borrowing method above using the examples below. Ensure that the child checks that the answer is correct using the multi-sensory method. If the child has any difficulty go back to an earlier point in the book and ensure that the process is fully understood before moving on.

A. $$\begin{array}{r} 46 \\ -28 \\ \hline \\ \hline \end{array} \quad \Longrightarrow \quad \begin{array}{r} 3^{1}6 \\ -2\ 8 \\ \hline 1\ 8 \\ \hline \end{array}$$

B. 62 ⇨ $5^{1}2$
-45 ⇨ -4 5

___ ___

1 7

___ ___

2. Having reached the conclusion that the child is comfortable with subtraction to this point ask him/her to do the following subtractions and set them out using both the mathematical method and the multi-sensory method. Watch closely as the child works as, if there are any mistakes made, you want to be able to pin point the exact stage at which the child went wrong.

   - 56 – 29 =
   - 31 – 24 =
   - 52 – 35 =
   - 98 – 29 =

Day 10.

1. With the child fully secure with subtraction up to 99, move on to dealing with numbers over 100. Set out 10 blue counters and ask the child what number they represent. Then ask if he/she remembers a simpler way of representing that number – the child should come up with 1 counter of another colour. In this book we use green, but of course the colour is not significant as long as it is different from the colours already used. If he/she does not remember/know this from Section 1 of the book you may want to go back and look at it together.

2. Ask the child to do the following subtractions using both the multi-sensory and mathematical methods.

   - 500 – 200 =
   - 300 – 200 =
   - 900 – 300 =
   - 700 – 400 =

   The child should be comfortable using 1 green counter to represent every 100. The child should be able to set the sums out in the mathematical format:

   500 300
   -200 -200

   ___ ___

   ___ ___

Day 11.

1. Ask the child to do the following subtraction using the multi-sensory method: 450 – 260 = ___. The problem arises here that the 60 on the bottom row cannot be taken away from the 50 on the top row. Remind the child that we can only take away red counters from red counters, blue from blue and green from green.

2. Ask the child for suggestions on how to tackle this subtraction.

   - We can take away the 0 red counters from the 0 red leaving 0 red.
   - We can take away the 2 green counters from the 4 green leaving 2 green.
   - But we cannot take 6 blue counters from 5 blue – it does not work.

   At this point remind the child that 1 green counter represents 10 blue counters and ask for any suggestions. He/she may suggest borrowing from the green counters by changing 1 green into 10 blue. At this point also introduce the concept of working form right to left which the child will already have met in the Addition Section of this book.

3. The child should demonstrate the following:

   - The original subtraction is 4 green, 5 blue and 0 red counters – 2 green, 6 blue and 0 red counters.
   - The units column does not cause a problem as 0 take away 0 is still 0.
   - But we cannot take away the 6 blue counters from the 5 blue – it does not work.
   - So we have to borrow from the green counters as we know that 1 green counter equals 10 blue counters. So 4 green and 5 blue counters can be converted to 3 green and 15 blue counters.
   - This would mean that we now start again with 3 green counters, 15 blue and 0 red – 2 green, 6 blue and 0 red.
   - This gives an answer of 1 green, 9 blue and 0 red - i.e. 190.

4. Remind the child that we can set this out as:

$$\begin{array}{r} 450 \\ -260 \\ \hline \\ \hline \end{array} \quad \Longrightarrow \quad \begin{array}{r} 3^{1}50 \\ -2\ 60 \\ \hline 1\ 90 \\ \hline \end{array}$$

Day 12.

1. Repeat points 2 and 3 from yesterday. Encourage the child to start at the right hand column first - ie with the red counters.

2. Ask the child to do the following subtractions using the mathematical method and to prove them using the multi-sensory method. If the child gets these correct move on to day 13, otherwise go back to Day 8 and revise until you are sure that the child fully understands what he/she is doing.

   - 350 – 260 =
   - 640 – 390 =
   - 910 – 650 =

Day 13.

1. Ask the child to do the subtraction 650 – 260 = ___ using both systems. If the child gets this correct move on to point 2.

2. Ask the child to do the subtraction 539 – 366 = ___. At this point the child is being asked to make calculations in all three columns – units, tens and hundreds. See if the child can do it him/herself first and watch carefully to see how it is tackled.

3. If the child has not got the answer correct to point 2 or has visibly struggled you may need to go back a few days and revise. Then go over it step by step in both the multi-sensory and the mathematical method.

4. Ask the child to set out the subtraction in counters so that he/she is touching the counters and talking about what he/she is doing at the same time:

    - 5 green, 3 blue and 9 red – 3 green, 6 blue and 6 red =
    - 9 red take away 6 red equals 3 red
    - 3 blue take away 6 blue cannot be done so we must borrow from the green counters by taking 1 green counter and exchanging it for 10 blue
    - We now have 13 blue take away 6 blue equals 7 blue
    - 4 green take away 3 green equals 1 green
    - The answer is 1 green, 7 blue and 3 red = 173

5. Go over the mathematical representation of this calculation.

6. Set some more examples to do, ensuring at this stage that only the tens column has a larger number on the bottom than on the top. Do not move on until you are sure that the child is entirely comfortable with both methods of calculation.

Day 14.

1. Ask the child to do the calculation 482 – 291 = ___. If the child gets the correct answer move on to point 2, otherwise go back over the previous day's work.

2. Ask the child to do the subtraction 654 – 266 = ___. This is the first time the child has had to do a subtraction where both the units and the tens in the top row are smaller than the units and tens in the bottom row. Do not rush the child and give him/her the chance to work this out.

3. If the child cannot do this remind him/her of how you solved the problem in point 1 and suggest that it is the same principle. Demonstrate it using counters, again allowing the child to touch the counters as you talk:

    - 6 green, 5 blue and 4 red counters have to become 5 green, 14 blue and 14 red before you can take away the 2 green, 6 blue and 6 red counters.

Day 15.

1. Revise point 2 from day 14. Give the child a few more examples to do using the counters.

2. If the child is getting the correct answers ask him or her to set it out in a mathematical way. Thus you should have:

$$\begin{array}{r} 654 \\ -\,266 \\ \hline \\ \hline \end{array} \quad \Longrightarrow \quad \begin{array}{r} 5\,{}^{1}4\,{}^{1}4 \\ -\,2\;6\;6 \\ \hline 3\;8\;8 \\ \hline \end{array}$$

Day 16.

1. Ask the child to do 5467 – 3628 = ___. Again take it slowly and explain that there is nothing new being asked here. If the child has understood the previous points you should be able to encourage him/her to do this successfully. Give some more examples to do and continue to use both the mathematical and multi-sensory methods.

Day 17 and onward.

By this time your child should have a good grasp of the methods used in subtraction and it is a case of coming back and revising regularly. When you feel that your child is ready you can encourage him/her only to use the mathematical method as this is clearly a much quicker way of reaching the same answer.

Activity 7

- Take a set of playing cards without the court cards and lay two out at random.
- Ask the child to arrange the larger number on the left and the smaller on the right.
- Now ask the child to subtract the card on the right from the one on the left. If the child finds this easy you can return the court cards to agree with the child that the Jack is worth 11, the Queen is 12, the King is 13.
- Give the child the whole pack and allow the child to lay down two cards, arrange them left and right and tell you the answer. The game is then to play yourself against the child (or have two children playing each other), with the winner being the highest answer (which would be King minus Ace – the ace in this game being worth one).

Activity 8

- Gather together a set of 101 cards and on each one write a number from 0 to 100.
- Give the child a selection of 2 cards at random.
- Once again the child has to take the higher from the lower. Again the game can be played as a competition with either the highest or the lowest answer winning.
- The game can be played over several rounds with the children keeping a record of their best and worst scores. The highest possible score would of course be 100, from 100 – 0, the lowest being the answer "1" which could come from any two consecutive numbers turning up. The game can be further enhanced by offering a small prize to the winner. Pen and paper is of course allowed to help the children get the right answer.

In both these games, if the children start making regular errors in the subtraction then a revision programme should be undertaken before the game is played again.

Table 5

First number	Second number	Answer

Table 6

First number	–	Second number	=	Answer

Table 7

First number	–	Second number	=	Answer

Part 4: Multi-sensory multiplication

Day 1.

1. Put a red counter on the table and give the child a pile of red counters for the activities that follow.

2. Tell the child you have one red counter on the table. Ask the child to put a second red counter down and say "two red counters." Continue this up to five.

3. Now put two red counters on the table, and the child says "two red counters." Now ask the child to add another group of two. The child puts down another group of two. Ask the child how many counters there are now on the table – the child should say four. Repeat the process with three sets of two, and the answer is six.

4. Now say to the child, "Put two counters on the table, and say 'one two is two.' 'One two' means you have one group of two counters on the table." The child should do it.

5. Now move to adding a second group of two counters. As the child puts them down the child should say, "two twos are four". Lay out the counters so that it is clear there are two groups of two.

6. Lay out three groups of two red counters. Ask the child how many groups there are. The answer is three. Ask the child what is in each group. The answer is two. Following the previous pattern the child now says, "three twos are six".

7. Continue up to 5 twos, unless the child is growing tired or is making mistakes.

Day 2.

1. The child should repeat yesterday's activities 4, 5, 6 and 7. Then if the child is able to cope with this satisfactorily, the child moves on to six twos, and so on up to 10.

2. Once the child can repeat the two times table in a multi-sensory form satisfactorily, then the child should repeat the exercise, but simultaneously write down the answers in Table 8 which is at the end of this section on page 60. So the child will write in the table:

How many groups	**x**	**What's in the group**	=	**Total**
3	x	2	=	6

3. Once the child can undertake the multi-sensory two times table ask the child to start again with the three times table. So you will start with one group with three in the group, then two groups with three in the group, and the child saying "one three is three, two threes are six". Once the child can recite the table as it is put down, up to five, the child should then repeat the exercise adding the numbers to the table.

Day 3.

1. Ask the child to draw a table like table 8 and repeat the three times table in multi-sensory form, including writing it in the table, up to five threes.

2. Now continue up to 10.

Day 4.

1. Revise the two and three times table with both the multi-sensory and the written form.

Day 5.

1. Work on the four times table in the same way as you have done with earlier tables. The child might be able to undertake the whole table in one go, or might want to take several days to do this, depending on the level of understanding.

2. At the end ask the child to look at the totals column of the four times table and the two times table. Is there any link? The answer is that the four times table contains every other total from the two times table – 4, 8, 12 and so on up to 20. After that it carries on building up with the right hand number – 24, 28, 32 and so on. Do remember that the point here is to generate an interest in numbers and the patterns that numbers form, rather than to get the child to learn a sequence.

Day 6.

1. Ask the child to consider the three tables, 2, 3 and 4, in terms of even and odd numbers. What is noticed? The answer is that the 2 and 4 times tables only include even numbers. And 2 and 4 are even numbers. The three times table contains alternating even and odd numbers – three is an odd number. Again what we are trying to do here is generate an interest in the fact that numbers do not appear randomly, but generate sequences.

2. Ask the child if she or he would make a prediction about odd and even numbers for the 5 times table. Will the answers in the table be:

   a) Random
   b) Alternating odd and even
   c) All odd
   d) All even

3. Ask the child to complete the work on the five times table, using the same technique as already established. At the end, compare the result with the prediction made yesterday. If the child is wrong, go over the problem and see why.

Day 7.

1. Tell the child we are going to work on the 6 times table today. Ask the child to predict the answers. Will they be:

   a) Random

b) Alternating odd and even
c) All odd
d) All even

Ask the child why.

2. Now ask the child if she or he can see any link between the three times table and the six times table. The answer should be of the same type as was found for the 2 and 4 times table – the 6 times table takes every other answer from the 3 times table.

3. Ask the child why this "every other answer effect" occurs. If the child does not know, put three counters on the table, and then another three, and ask how many there are. Repeat this, taking the total to 9 and 12. Ask what the relation is between three and six. The answer should be that six is two threes, 12 is four threes. Repeat this with two and four.

Day 8.

1. Create the six times table as has been done with other tables, and check the predictions made yesterday. If any of the predictions are wrong, look with the child to see how this error was made. Ideally the child should spot the error and be able to see where she or he has gone wrong.

Day 9.

1. Move on to the 7 times table, working as before. Ask the child to predict the answers. Will they be:

   a) Random
   b) Alternating odd and even
   c) All odd
   d) All even

   Ask the child why he/she is making this prediction.

2. Write out the 7 times table following the pattern used before.

3. Now ask the child if she or he can see any link between the 7 times table and any other. The answer should be no, apart from the answers alternating even and odd, there is no link.

Day 10.

1. Move on to the 8 times table. Ask the child to predict the answers. Will they be:

   a. Random
   b. Alternating odd and even
   c. All odd
   d. All even

   Ask the child why he/she is making this prediction.

2. Now ask the child if she or he can see any link between the eight times table and any other table. The answer should be that the 8 times table takes every other answer from the 4 times table. Once this is established write out the table.

3. Ask the child why this "every other answer effect" occurs. If the child does not know, put four counters on the table, and then another four, and ask how many there are. Ask what the relationship is between four and eight. The answer should be that eight is two fours.

Day 11

1. Move on to the 9 times table. Ask the child to predict the answers. Will they be:

   a) Random
   b) Alternating odd and even
   c) All odd
   d) All even.

   Ask the child why this prediction is made, and then complete the table.

2. When the child has completed the table, ask the child if she or he can see any link between the numbers. The answer should be that there is a pattern in the answers – the left number rises and the right number declines. In addition, the pair of numbers always adds up to 9.

9	$0 + 9 = 9$
18	$1 + 8 = 9$
27	$2 + 7 = 9$
36	$3 + 6 = 9$
45	$4 + 5 = 9$
54	$5 + 4 = 9$
63	$6 + 3 = 9$
72	$7 + 2 = 9$
81	$8 + 1 = 9$
90	$9 + 0 = 9$

Day 12.

1. Ask the child to work with the 10 times table and set out the answers mathematically and in a multi-sensory way. The child should be able to work through the whole process, making predictions, writing out the table, saying the table, and then drawing out interesting points – in this case that the answer always ends in zero.

   For the multi-sensory element of the 10 times table, you can use ten red counters or one blue counter. Ask the child to lay out and say the table both ways. The statements will be the same either way – "one ten is ten" etc - but in one case the child will gradually be moving around 100 red counters, in the other case, he or she will be moving 10 blue counters.

Day 13.

1. Now ask the child to handle the 11 times table. Ask for the usual predictions – and note that the predictions should be the same – there is no change just because the number being multiplied is over 10.

   In working in the multi-sensory approach the child should be putting down one red and one blue counter for each 11. Thus 33 is represented by three blues and three reds. The child should be able to look at this combination of red and blue and see the answer at once – if not, you should return to the earlier work on numbers to secure this awareness. The child should have no problem doing the table in a multi-sensory way because all he or she has to do is put down one more counter of each colour and see what the result is.

Day 14.

1. The 12 times table presents an extra problem. With the multi-sensory version the child puts down one blue and two red counters for each extra twelve. This is easy, except that when the child gets to 5 x 12 = 60, he or she will actually have 5 blues (50) and 10 reds (10). Ask the child to count the reds, and on finding there is a 10, pile them into a pile of 10. Ask the child what we normally do with a 10 – the answer is that we change the 10 reds for a blue. This can be done, and now there are six blues – for sixty. So five twelves are six blues (60).

2. Now carry on – the next multiplication is easy – we add a blue and two reds – six twelves equals seven blues plus 2 reds (72). At 8 x 12 the child should have 9 blues and 6 reds which obviously is 96.

3. The next problem arises at 9 x 12. Here the child has 10 blues and 8 reds. A pile of tens is always a warning – we have to translate it into something else. Using the number system we developed in section 1 of this book, ten blues equals a green, and the child should trade in the blues for a green. The child now sees one green (100) and 8 reds (8) = 108.

4. There is a further problem with 10 x 12. The child now is faced with one green, one blue and 10 reds. The 10 reds can be traded for another blue, giving one green (100) and two blues (20) = 120.

Day 15.

1. There is no need to stop at 12, as the multi-sensory approach to multiplication works just as well with higher numbers. Without suggesting that this next stage is any different ask the child to work on the 13 times table, not forgetting the transformations of reds into blues and blues into greens.

Day 16.

1. Give the child a piece of paper on which it says:

$$\begin{array}{r} 13 \\ \times\ 8 \\ \hline \\ \hline \end{array}$$

The child will know that "x" means the interaction between the number in the group and the number of groups. Tell the child that you normally call "x" "times". So we have here the question "what is 13 times 8?"

Ask the child to work in a multi-sensory way, and calculate 13 x 8. This can be done by adding blue and red counters and trading in the groups of 10 reds for blues.

2. Now ask the child if there is a way of working out the mathematical solution to:

$$\begin{array}{r} 13 \\ \times\ 8 \\ \hline \\ \hline \end{array}$$

without using the multi-sensory approach.

The child should puzzle this through and search for a method which produces the correct answer, 104. Clearly adding up the numbers 13 and 8 doesn't work, but adding up 13 eight times does work, although this is cumbersome.

3. What we need is for the child to realise that 3 x 8 = 24, which gives a 4 on the right hand side - exactly as the multi-sensory answer gives.

So you might now have a calculation that looks like this:

$$\begin{array}{r} 13 \\ \times\ 8 \\ \hline 24 \\ \hline \end{array}$$

Now the problem arises as to what happens with the 8 and the 1. The child's reaction might well be 8 x 1 = 8 – but no matter where the 8 is put in it won't give us 104.

If the child is stuck here ask the child how that 13 at the top would be represented in a multi-sensory way. The answer is one blue and three reds. Ask the child what the blue stands for – the answer is 10. So if we multiply the 1 (from 13) and the 8 we are not multiplying together 1 x 8, but rather 10 x 8. What is the answer to 10 x 8?

The child should be able to get to 80 for this – if not go back to the 10 times table and revise that.

Now tell the child we have two answers so far. We have 3 x 8 = 24 and 10 x 8 = 80.

Is there any way in which 24 and 80 can work together to get 104, which the multi-sensory approach tells us is the correct answer.

The answer is we add them together.

Day 17.

1. Repeat 13 x 8 both as a multi-sensory and as a mathematical calculation.

2. Now ask the child to work out 13 x 7 both as a multi-sensory and as a mathematical calculation, showing all the workings in the mathematical calculation. If the child cannot do this, help the child through the steps as yesterday. If the child can do it, you can move on to Day 18.

Day 18.

1. Ask the child to work out 13 x 4, 13 x 6 and 13 x 9 in both multi-sensory and mathematical ways.

Day 19.

1. Ask the child to work out 14 x 4, 14 x 7 and 14 x 6 in both a multi-sensory and a mathematical way.

Day 20.

1. Continue with this process working with 15 x 5, 16 x 3, 17 x 6 and 18 x 4.

Day 21.

1. Ask the child to multiply 20 x 10, 20 x 20, 20 x 30, 30 x 40 and 50 x 10. Ask the child to look for a short cut so that he or she does not have to work out each question in either a multi-sensory or mathematical way. The answer of course is that if you are multiplying by a number with a zero at the end you just add a zero to the answer for the rest of the question. 20 x 30 is the same as 2 x 3 with a nought added to the answer for each nought in the question. There is a 0 in 20 and another 0 in 30. So we have two noughts, and need to add two noughts into the answer.

2. If the child does not grasp this, take the question 20 x 20 and ask the child to work out the answer using the multi-sensory technique, and then work out an answer mathematically. Repeat with other questions for this list.

Day 22.

1. Ask the child to multiply 6 x 8 using the multi-sensory method.

2. Now ask the child to multiple 8 x 6 in the same way. What does he or she notice about the answers? Obviously they are the same.

3. Ask the child to repeat this exercise with 9 x 3 and 3 x 9.

4. From these answers ask the child to make up a rule that is always going to hold good. (The answer is that in multiplication it does not matter which way around the numbers are presented – the answer is always the same. 9 x 3 is the same as 3 x 9.)

5. Ask the child if this same rule applies to addition. Try it with 9 + 3 and 3 + 9. What rule can the child now make?

6. Finally ask the child if this applies to subtraction. Is 9 – 3 the same as 3 – 9? The answer is no. So the overall rule is that in addition and multiplication, the order of the numbers doesn't make any difference. But in subtraction the order of the numbers is essential.

Day 23.

1. Ask the child to multiply 18 x 25. Using the multi-sensory method this should cause no problems – the answer will be four greens and five blues, representing 450. The only problem is that it can take quite a long time to get there.

2. Next the child has to work it out in a mathematical calculation. Set the work out for the child like this:

```
  18
x 25
____

____
```

   The child will know that she or he has to get an answer of 450 – but how? The work on earlier, smaller multiplications should help.

   At this stage we would expect the child to multiply 8 x 5 to give 40 – which has a zero at the end, exactly as the multi-sensory answer does.

3. What we now have to try and do is persuade the child to multiply all the other numbers by each other while remembering that numbers on the left are 10s and not units.

   This can be very complex for a child, so if the child is having problems at this point, try a new approach. Write out the multiplication in various steps. 18 x 25 can be broken down into four steps:

   5 x 8 (the two right hand numbers)
   5 x 10 (one right one left)
   20 x 8 (one left one right)
   20 x 10 (the two left hand numbers)

   What must be remembered is that every left hand number is actually a blue counter – a certain number of 10s.

4. If this is still not clear to the child, then return to the multi-sensory method.

At the end, whichever method is to be used, the totals need to be added together to give the child the answer.

Day 24.

1. Return to:

```
  18
x 25
____

____
```

and ask the child to work this through. The child needs to remember three things:

a) that each number must be multiplied by both the numbers in the other line
b) that the left hand numbers are 10s – they are like blue counters
c) that the results need to be added together.

Day 25 and beyond.

Ask the child to multiply 17 x 24, using both methods. Ask him or her to ensure that the answers come out the same each time and that, when the mathematical method is used, the working is clearly shown.

From here on the process remains the same – it is now a matter of getting the child to practise multiplications using both the multi-sensory approach and the mathematical approach. Initially only set the child multiplications where the answer comes out at 999 or less. When you feel the child is ready, ask him or her to do questions where the answers lie between 1000 and 9999. The multi-sensory approach should still work because all the child has to do is exchange 10 reds for a blue, 10 blues for a green and 10 greens for a yellow at each stage in the calculation. But the child will learn quickly that the multi-sensory method, although accurate, is time consuming and cumbersome when the numbers become large. So a time will come where the child does not want to verify one method against the other.

At this point and if you feel that there is a fair chance of the child getting the right answer you can allow the child to work on just the mathematical method.

Activity 9

- Take your pack of numbered cards from 0 to 10 and give the child two at random.
- The child has to multiply these two together either mentally or using pen and paper.
- This game can be played between two children. Because numbers come out randomly, and because we anticipate that the children will get each answer right by this stage, the game's scoring system is based on the size of the answer. Answers between 0 and 9 win one point. Answers between 10 and 19 win two points. Answers between 20 and 29 win three points and so on up to answers between 90 and 99 which win 10 points each. Assuming that you only have one card for each number the highest answer will be 10 x 9 which is 90.
- The game can be extended by having two cards for each number, which then means that the highest answer would be the unique 10 x 10, which could gain 11 points.

- Play 10 rounds and then total up who wins.

Activity 10

- Take a pack of numbered cards from 0 to 100 and give the child two at random.
- The child has to multiply these two together.
- Again two children can play each other, but this time the scoring system should be: answers between 10, no score, thereafter the score is equal to the value of 10s – so 21 x 35 = 735 which is 73 points. Adding the points up at the end will be a good revision of the addition work undertaken earlier.
- Give lots of prizes!

Table 8

How many groups	x	What's in the group	=	Total

Section 5: Multi-sensory division

Day 1

1. Put six red counters on the table and tell the child that we want to divide them in two. It is important to use the phrase "divide into two" rather than "divide in half" or "split in half" or "cut in half". The child should be able to work out that there should be two piles of three. If not, you can say to the child, "Let's work this out step by step. Put one counter on this side, and one on that. Now let's do it again." After the third division into two, there are no counters left, and so you have three in each pile. Tell the child that you have just divided the six counters into two. How many are there in each group?

2. Repeat the exercise with eight counters and then ten counters. If there are problems in understanding this work, repeat the exercise.

3. Now ask the child to repeat these three divisions, to say what is happening and to write down the answers in table 9 at the end of this section on page 67. The table will look like this:

How many counters to start with?	÷	**How many groups are they divided into?**	=	**How many are there per group?**
6	÷	2	=	3
8	÷	2	=	4
10	÷	2	=	5

Day 2.

1. Tell the child to count out six red counters. Ask the child to divide them into two groups as per yesterday and to say what is happening as he/she goes along.

2. Repeat the activity but this time ask for the six counters to be divided into three groups. Complete table 9 with the result.

3. Repeat the activity with 8 counters divided into 2 groups and 4 groups.

Day 3.

1. Draw up a new copy of the division chart. Place 2 counters on the table, and ask the child to divide them into 2 groups. The answer of course is that there will be one counter in each group. The child must physically move the counters, say what is being done, write the answer on the chart and, in writing it down, say "Two divided by two equals one" – which is exactly the sequence that the chart shows.

2. Move on to 4 red counters and again divide into 2 groups. You can point out to the child that this exercise is all about dividing into two groups. If the child is not at all confused by this work, point out that people often call dividing into two groups "divided by two".

3. As long as the child is getting the answers right keep going with 6, 8 and 10 – but don't go further. At "10 divided into 2" use 10 red counters and complete the exercise. Then ask the child for another way of expressing "10" in multi-sensory work. The answer should be one blue counter. The child should then look at the one blue counter, and replace it by 10 reds and then split them into the two groups.

4. Now move onto 12 – represented by 1 blue and 2 reds. To make this work the child is going to have to replace the blue with 10 reds, and then split – there is no other way of achieving a result, short of cutting the blue in half, and that is strictly not allowed!

5. Continue to 20. The child should immediately see that for the first time the two blues do not have to be changed to reds – you can simply put one in each of the two piles.

Day 4

1. Repeat points 4 and 5 from yesterday.

2. Now ask the child to look at dividing 22 into 2. Again no transforming is required since one blue and one red can go into each group.

3. Continue to 30. At 30, one of the 3 blues will need to be exchanged for reds. The point of this exercise is that the child needs to consider each situation and see what should be done – there isn't an automatic rule, except for the fact that if the number of blues is even, and you are dividing by an even number, then no transformation is needed. This however is not likely to help the child – so we leave it that there is no rule.

Day 5

1. Repeat the division into 2 of numbers 22 to 30 from yesterday (point 3).

2. Put out three red counters and tell the child that you are dividing into 3 groups. The same process works as per yesterday with the child using both multi-sensory and mathematical representation, as well as handling, writing and speaking the numbers.

3. Put out 6 counters, then 9 and 12. At 12 the child should remember that the blue needs to be transformed into 10 reds.

4. Continue through 15, 18 and 21. At 21 the child might make the assumption that the two blues can be split, but of course this can't happen because we have three groups – the two blues must become 20 reds.

5. Continue until 30. At 30, at long last, the three blues can be split between the three groups.

Day 6

1. Repeat point 5 from yesterday.

2. Continue until 42. From 30 to 39 the groups can be split easily without changing blues into reds, but at 42 one of the blues must be split. If the child does not see this immediately, then remind the child of what happened at 30. Since you still have 3 blues on the table you can divide these up, and then deal with the 12 remaining.

3. Start again with a new chart. This time you are dividing into 4 groups, which you might remind the child is often called "divided into 4".

4. Work through the table to 40. The child should now be getting the idea that sometimes blues have to be transformed into reds – but not always.

Day 7

1. Work through division into groups of 5.

2. When you have completed the divisions up to 50 ask the child if he or she sees any pattern in the numbers in the left column. It should be clear that these all end with 0 and 5.

3. Now ask the child if there was any pattern with the divide into 4 chart. The answer is that the numbers we divided are all even and fall into a pattern with the last number running 4, 8, 2, 6, 0. This of course is the same as the pattern found in the multiplication section under 4. If the child does not recall this, or did not do the multiplication section, sit down with the child and look for patterns in dividing into 2 groups and 3 groups. Of course these patterns only show up if we are dividing numbers which give whole number answers. The child does not need to know this, but if thc issuc is raised, allow the child to see the problem. 7 divided into 2 groups allows you divide up 6 of the numbers with 3 in each group but what do you do with the 7th? The answer is split it in half – and this is better left until later.

Day 8

1. Work through division into groups of 6. If the child is moving rapidly through this, look for patterns, and move straight on to 7s.

Day 9

1. Continue working through the numbers – if 7 was done yesterday continue with 8, and then 9.

Day 10

1. Dividing into groups of 10 is interesting because it shows the simplicity of the use of the zero and the transfer from red to blue. You put out just blue counters, and the division is simple. The mathematical representation is equally simple. You can also try dividing by 11 as soon as dividing by 10 is mastered.

2. You can move onto 12 and continue upwards. We do not expect children to learn divisions into groups of these higher numbers but we do expect the children to be able to handle these numbers. As the numbers being divided are already moving over 100 and the child has experience of transferring red to blue and blue to green and back again, these multi-sensory transformations should cause no problems. What will cause a problem will be division using a mathematical method. We therefore need to set these higher number problems to help the child to find a mathematical solution to division. Don't move on from this point until you are happy that the child can handle the types of division undertaken thus far.

Day 11

1. Ask the child to divide 210 into 14 – that is to divide 2 greens and 1 blue. The answer is 15.

2. Ask the child how this can be done mathematically – and much more rapidly – without relying on the multi-sensory method. Discuss this with the child.

3. If the child comes up with a system that works, that is fine. Set some more problems of a similar nature, and ask the child to try this out without using multi-sensory techniques, to check that the system works.

4. If the system fails or if the child does not come up with a system, help the child by going back to a much simpler problem. Ask the child how we could divide 12 into 3 groups and know how many there were in each group, using maths? The answer is that somehow we have to know how many times three fits into 12. This is not too hard because we can lay out groups of three counters until we get to 12, or we can take 12 counters and keep putting one in each group of three and find however many counters there are in each group. Either way gives us 4. But how about 210 divided into 14?

   If there is still no answer ask the child to try this:

   - We are asking how many groups of 14 there are in 210. Rather than try to tackle the whole of 210 as a big number, let's start from the left. How many 14s are there in 2? The child should see immediately that the answer is none – 2 is a tiny number and 14 is a bigger number.

   - If the child is bemused by this, clear the table of counters, and then say, how many groups of 14 do we have. The answer is 0. Put down 14 red counters and ask the question. The answer is that we have 1 group of 14. Put down 5 counters, and ask again. The answer must be none because when you count to five there are still not enough to make 14. If the child does not seem to fully grasp this, abandon 210 divided 14 and repeat this question of how many groups of x are there in y. Just work through any numbers you want – but always check that the answer will come out as a whole number or zero. Thus you could have 63 divided by 9 and 8 divided by 9, but not 12 divided by 9.

Day 12

1. Revise the work from yesterday so that the child is reminded of the problem being tackled.

2. Assuming now that the child can answer the question "How many 14s are there in 2?" and get the answer 0, now proceed both mathematically and using the multi-sensory method

   - How many groups of 14 are there in 210? – this is too big a problem, we'll break it down by starting from the left of the big number we are looking to break up into groups of 14. And we are going to look at a mathematical way of writing it:

     $14\overline{)210}$ How many groups of 14 are there in 2 – none.

   - That didn't get us anywhere, so let's try the first two numbers – 21. Put down 21 red counters, and divide them into groups of 14. What happens? The answer is that you get one group of 14, but you have 7 left over. So looking at our maths again you would get this:

     $$\begin{array}{r} 1 \\ 14\overline{)210} \end{array}$$

     But where are we going to put those 7 that are left over?

     Here the child can experiment, and if the child goes down the wrong route it does not matter too much because the answer is going to be validated by the multi-sensory method.

   - The only way to make this work is to put the 7 in front of the 0 from 210. You now have the number "70". The question now is how many 14s are there in 70. If the child has no idea how to approach this, ask the child to set out 14 in counters and write down 14 (this would be one blue and four red counters in the multi-sensory approach).

   - Then ask the child to lay down another 14 counters, and then add the two groups together, to get the answer 28. Remind the child you have two groups of 14 counters and have got 28 (two blue and 8 red) in total.

   - Now repeat the process once more, adding a third group of 14 counters, which gives us 42.

   - A further repeat of the process gives 56, and one more – the 5th run gives a total of 70. Which shows that there are 5 groups of 14 counters in 70 counters. There are five 14s in 70.

   - We can now look again at the complete division problem.

     $$\begin{array}{r} 15 \\ 14\overline{)210} \end{array}$$

     The answer is 15.

Day 13

1. There is an alternative approach available in which the question is answered as a whole. The issue of how many 14s are there in 210 is faced directly.

2. 14 counters (i.e. one blue and four red) are placed down and the number 14 is written down, with the number of groups next to it as in the table overleaf:

Number per group	No of groups of 14	Total
14	1	14
14	2	28
14	3	42
14	4	56

This process continues until the student gets to 210 and finds there are 15.

3. If the child is having real problems understanding the approach in the previous day, give the child this alternative method. This will only be a temporary solution, but is worth considering because it unblocks a particular problem. The difficulty will return when the problems get very big – such as how many 16s there are in 1,584.

Activity 9

- Create a set of cards with one card for each of these numbers: 14, 28, 42, 56, 70, 84, 98, 112, 126, 140, 154, 168, 182, 196, 210, 224, 238, 252, 266, 280, 294, 308.
- Now ask the child or children playing the game to turn up one card. They then have to work out how many 14s there are in the total that comes up.
- You can score 1 point for an answer up to 9; 2 points for an answer up to 19; 3 points for above.
- You can extend the series as far as you like to give more variety to the game.

Activity 10

- Repeat game 9 but this time use a set of cards reflecting the 16 times table (16, 32, 48, 64, 80, 96, 112, 128, 144, 160, 176, 192, 208, 224, 240, 256, 272, 288, 304, 320, 336, 352, 368 etc)

Activity 11

- Repeat game 9 but this time use a set of cards reflecting the 17 times table (17, 34, 51, 68, 85, 102, 119, 136, 153, 170, 187, 204, 221, 238, 255, 272, 289, 306, 323, 340, 357, 374, 391, 408 etc)

Activity 12

- Now you have three sets of cards established create a second set with just 3 cards in it (14, 16, and 17)
- The child chooses one of those three cards, which then dictates which larger pack is chosen. So if the child selects the card "17" the child then has to pick a card from the set that runs 17, 34, 51 etc.
- This series of games can continue by adding other sets for other numbers – 13, 15, 18 and so on.

Table 9

How many counters to start with?	÷	How many groups are they divided into?	=	How many are there per group?
	÷		=	
	÷		=	
	÷		=	
	÷		=	
	÷		=	
	÷		=	
	÷		=	
	÷		=	
	÷		=	
	÷		=	
	÷		=	
	÷		=	